# The Procrastinator's Paper Pile Solution

The Easy, Little-Steps Guide To
Decluttering Paper
(Without Complicated
Decision-Making Or Long
Attention Spans)

By Nealey Stapleton

# Table Of Contents

# <u>Introduction</u>

(You pick up a piece of paper…)

You look at it, you get frustrated and then you put that darn thing back down on the pile and walk away overwhelmed. You think to yourself, "I've got so many other priorities that I could be dealing with right now rather than this silly, confusing piece of paper."

But then, every time you pass that pile (or piles) of paper your stomach turns. The sight of the clutter is driving you nuts. What if there's something important in that document mountain? What if there isn't and the entire thing can be recycled?

It's just paper, and you're a high functioning human being. For heaven's sake, you (insert one of your awesome accomplishments here)! How is it getting the best of you? No, you won't stand for this intrusion any longer. You pick up a piece of paper…ugh!

Sound familiar?

Well, I'm here to help you break that brick wall of a procrastination cycle and teach you how to do it over and over again. By the time your finished with this book, you'll OWN that procrastination. It's going to be the one begging for mercy!

Before I get carried away though, here are a few quick things about me (so you know who it is giving you this awesome advice). My name is Nealey Stapleton, and it's a pleasure to meet you. In short, I'm a professional organizer, an author, a small business owner, a DIY blogger, an adoring wife, a Pug lover, a hula hooping guru, a cheese addict and a happy napper.

I've been responsible for organizing myself since…well, birth. My mom claims that as a baby I would remove my own dirty diaper in the middle of the night, fold it up neatly and put it in the corner of the crib. After all, it had been used and had no business staying on my body, so I put it where it belonged. LOL!

I've been helping people get organized since I was 5. Yes, 5! Those were the days when my grandparents' mountain of shoes needed my help, and when I was done they were arranged by size and color.

I could go on and on about similar stories as I grew up, but let's fast forward to today. I've been helping people get organized and bust through their procrastination professionally since 2007. That's where this book comes in. The tips you will read here have worked for my clients (as well as myself – my life gets messy and procrastination-ridden too) and I know they can work for you.

I'm excited about helping you, so back to breaking the brick wall of the procrastination cycle. Let's. Do. This. (Queue the music - a song that inspires you and gets you going. My first thought was We Will Rock You by Queen. Boom boom bah!)

Go back to that piece of paper on top of that pile. Pick it up. Just that one piece of paper and nothing else. What is it? Say it out loud. Where does it go? Now, STOP.

If you are stuck here, then don't give up and walk away (which is one of the most common ways the ugly procrastination monster rears his ugly head. Don't let him win.). Your next step, rather, is to put words as to why you don't know what to do with the paper.

Is it tax-related? Is it reminding you to do something? Is it something you know you need to keep but don't know how to file it? Is it something you want to get rid of but not sure if you should recycle or shred it? Is it a memory?

What's your question? Say it out loud. Once you verbalize it, then you know what it is you need to find out and therefore what your next step is. Breaking down the project into these micro steps has worked repeatedly for my clients and myself, and I know it can work for you too.

Typically, your question can be answered by doing a simple Google search but the awesome thing is that you're reading this right now. You don't need to go anywhere for the time being; keep reading and your paper organizing questions will be answered.

This guide is meant to take the overwhelming nature of organizing paper out of the process. There is no fluff here; who wants clutter in an organizing book anyway?!

This is straight up how-to information

that gets results AS LONG AS YOU
TAKE ACTION. I can't emphasize
that enough. It can be teeny tiny
action steps, but as long as they are
consistent you will be way ahead of
where you were.

This book is laid out in individual
small tips that are easy to
understand and powerful in their own
rite, but also work together
cohesively. It is a lot of information to
digest all in one sitting, but if you do
read the book cover to cover then
understand that this is a reference
book for you to come back to as
much as you need.

Also, at the end there is a link to a
one-page cheat sheet that you can
download for free. Keep it on hand
as you organize your paper, rather
than having to go back and flip
through all the pages in this book.

When you finish reading, my
suggestion is to schedule a block of
time (preferably a short 15-30 minute

session) in the next week to start on ONE tip. You can start with the first tip or wherever makes sense for your personal situation. When the 15-30 minutes is up, stop. Then schedule the next session on your calendar and come back to continue on. This progresses your paper organizing forward and also prevents burn out.

If it helps, put on motivating background music or light a scented candle. Feeling good and relaxed while you are sorting through paper will improve the experience. This will help with keeping the procrastination at bay the next time you need to organize paper. For an activity that is essentially a never-ending task (because there will always be paper to sort through), staying motivated is key.

Ready? Let's rock this together.

# **DECLUTTERING**

(Because it feels so good.)

# <u>Tip #1</u>

DECLUTTERING

There are 2 things you can do with a piece of paper – you can keep it or discard it. I know this is obvious, but for those who find decision-making a pain, it's important to make clear-cut lines in the sand. The next time you have a piece of paper in your hand, the first question is if you need to keep it or discard it. Then go from there.

# <u>Tip #2</u>

DECLUTTERING

When sorting through paper during a decluttering session, do NOT put a piece of paper back down on the pile. That's the paper organizing kiss of death.

Follow this straightforward process:

Say out loud what it is, what questions you have if any, decide if you need to keep it and put it where it belongs. (Don't worry, we'll be addressing the questions you may have and "where it belongs" part in detail.)

# <u>Tip #3</u>

DECLUTTERING

If you have questions and are unsure of whether or not you need to keep the piece of paper, then here are some guidelines for figuring out how to make that decision.

First, look it up online. Do a quick search on Google or whatever search engine you use with the following phrase, "how long to keep fill-in-the-blank" (e.g. bank statements, tax records, investment confirmations).

Second, ask a trusted expert. If it's a tax document, ask your accountant. Legal document? Ask a lawyer and so on.

Third, do you have access to a digital copy of this document? Whether it's something like an online bank statement or something simple like a recipe that you can look back up, then you can probably let go of the physical paper.

Fourth, if you're thinking, "what if I need this after I get rid of it?" then ask yourself what's the worst that could happen by not having it. Is there a way to retrieve the information? Yes? It can go. No? Keep it.

# Tip #4

DECLUTTERING

If you know you need to keep it but don't know where the piece of paper belongs, then a home must be created for it. Refer to the next section for straightforward instructions on how to do this depending on what it is.

# <u>Tip #5</u>

DECLUTTERING

Do the decluttering session mentioned in #2 for 15 minutes consistently until your paper piles disappear. It doesn't have to be every day; it could be every weekday, every other day or whatever works for you. It just has to be on a regular basis.

# <u>Tip #6</u>

DECLUTTERING

Schedule these consistent blocks of time on your calendar. If you use a digital calendar, then you can set up a repeating event with an alarm that sounds when it's time to start.

For example, you could have a repeating event on your digital calendar that goes off every Monday morning at 9am when the house is quiet, you've had your coffee and you're feeling productive.

# <u>Tip #7</u>

DECLUTTERING

Make it easier on yourself to commit to those 15 minutes by setting a timer or creating a music playlist of 5-7 songs. When the alarm rings or the playlist is over, you are done. It's important to stop when the allotted time is up, so that you remember how quickly the time went and will be motivated to come back the next time.

# <u>Tip #8</u>

DECLUTTERING

If the piece of paper in your hand is a discard and has identifying personal information on it, then shred it. Identifying personal information tends to be numbers like birth dates, account numbers, social security numbers and so on. <u>For a more detailed list of papers to shred, go to https://www.the-organizing-boutique.com/shredding-paper.html.</u>

# <u>Tip #9</u>

DECLUTTERING

If the piece of paper in your hand is a discard and doesn't have identifying personal information on it, then recycle it.

# <u>Tip #10</u>

DECLUTTERING

Be sure to have strategically-placed receptacles around your house to make this as easy as possible. I have found that having labeled "recycle" bins on each level to be very convenient. Also, keep a shredder in a handy spot like near your mail sorting station or wherever you go through your mail.

# Tip #11

DECLUTTERING

It must be said that most people don't like going through paper, myself included, so don't be too hard on yourself. That kind of self-discouragement can be a huge detriment. Just remember, the difference between those who procrastinate and those who actually get it done is consistent action. I know I said this earlier but it's definitely worth repeating.

If you feel the procrastination monster starting to rear his ugly head (check out https://www.the-organizing-boutique.com/ways-to-avoid-procrastination.html), then take a micro step in the right direction. Sort for 5 minutes if you can't do 15 right now or simply find the answer to whatever question is keeping you from going forward. Just do something small so that there's progress, and then come back tomorrow.

# A Note From The Author

**To jump right in and bust through those paper piles, download the paper decluttering cheat sheet that supplements this book for free at https://www.the-organizing-boutique.com/paper-decluttering-cheat-sheet.html.**

Hey there! Did you enjoy this book? My hope is that you found it interesting, useful and motivating.

When I set out to write this book, my goal was to help people get through those paralyzing paper piles successfully by breaking down such an overwhelming project into doable, bite-sized tasks that can be immediately applied. Whether you got that out of reading this guide or you simply have one awesome takeaway, I'd love to hear about it.

I would kindly like to ask you to leave me an honest Amazon review. It can be short and sweet. Simply state one thought or feeling you took away after reading this book. Doing so not only spreads the word (which I immensely appreciate), but it also increases the possibility of helping someone else.

Thanks in advance and happy organizing!

# STORAGE

(If not, you end up with those
overwhelming piles.)

# Tip #12

STORAGE

Once you've decided to keep a piece of paper, there are 3 categories it could fall into:

1. Action
2. Current
3. Archival

# Tip #13

STORAGE

This must be said early, so it doesn't bog you down later. You don't need fancy labels or stylish folders. Get organized with what you have, and then you can go back later and spiff it up. Being organized can be very pretty, but it doesn't have to be. It just needs to be functional, so let's take that "perfection" pressure off right now.

# <u>Tip #14</u>

STORAGE > ACTION

Action items refer to things like bills, invitations that need responses, tasks to complete, phone calls to make and so on. In short, they require you to take some sort of action.

# Tip #15

STORAGE > ACTION

Action items need to have a home, so you have a place to put them and need to be in plain sight to serve as a visual reminder. For example, this could be a paper tray on your desk or a magazine file on your kitchen counter.

# Tip #16

STORAGE > ACTION

Organize action items by date with an accordion file, by category (bills, invitations, etc.) using stacking letter trays or by how long it will take to complete them (e.g. less than 10 minutes, more than 10 minutes, more than 30 minutes). For more details like product suggestions, go to https://www.the-organizing-boutique.com/monthly-bill-organizer.html.

# Tip #17

STORAGE > ACTION

Schedule action items on your calendar as well as take into account deadlines and due dates. If your action pile becomes too big and overwhelming, it will be another stack of ignored paper. You can either schedule each individual item on your calendar or block off a certain amount of time every day to tend to your action items.

# Tip #18

STORAGE > ACTION

The action papers need to be looked through every day. I highly recommend you check in with your action papers each morning, so that you don't overlook something urgent.

# Tip #19

STORAGE > ACTION

Once the action item has been taken care of, the paper needs to be processed accordingly. If you no longer need it, then shred it or recycle it. If it something to keep, then file it appropriately. Filing options are addressed in the next section.

# <u>Tip #20</u>

STORAGE > ACTION

Using these tips, your action papers shouldn't become an overwhelming and toppling pile. If they do, however, then it's time to go through and assess if there are any action items you can delegate or turn down.

# Tip #21

STORAGE > ACTION

Another reason action piles could become too big is if they are full of paper that is reminding you to do something.

For example, a piece of paper with a phone number on it that is reminding you to call that person shouldn't be in the action pile. That name and number should be on your to do list and/or scheduled in your calendar, and the paper should be recycled. If you need to keep that phone number, then enter it into your contacts application or address book and then recycle it.

Go through your action pile and take out any paper that falls into this category and process it accordingly.

# <u>Tip #22</u>

STORAGE > ACTION

One last category of items that tend to end up in the action pile and take up a lot of room are the papers that would be considered "things to read." This refers to things like magazines, catalogs and other leisure reading.

Rather than exponentially growing the action pile and becoming overwhelmed, pick a location or home for your reading items that works with your habits.

For example, I do a lot of my reading on the couch in the living room. When reading materials come in through the mail or what have you, I place them on the coffee table and read through them that week. Since it's such a visible location, I remember to actually read them and I'm also encouraged to keep the pile small or nonexistent so it doesn't look cluttered.

# <u>Tip #23</u>

STORAGE > CURRENT

The next category of paper to file includes documents that are current.

Current papers are relevant now (so they can't be discarded yet), but will expire or become obsolete once an event passes, someone else does their part of the required action and so on.

For instance, they could be paid bills, work projects, current tax year files, manuals, papers pending the action of others, concert tickets and so on.

# Tip #24

STORAGE > CURRENT >
PENDING

One type that falls into the current category are the pending papers. You've done your required action in relation to these papers and are now waiting for someone else to do their part or waiting for the event to pass.

# Tip #25

STORAGE > CURRENT > PENDING

It's important to have a system in place for processing these pending papers, so that you complete your part, you remember to follow up if necessary and you can find them easily. It can be as simple as following the 3-step system in the next tip.

# Tip #26

STORAGE > CURRENT >
PENDING

**The first step is processing the piece of paper that comes in** and doing your required action. Let's say an invitation comes in the mail, and then your required action is to decide if you want to or are able to attend and RSVP.

**The second step is to add the event to your calendar,** and include any special notes, reminders and/or follow-ups. For example, if the invitation were for a wedding, you'd put the event date in your calendar as well as a reminder to get a card and a gift.

**The third step is to store the paper** and any related material together in a place that is easy to access like a nearby desk file drawer, a binder or a desktop file sorter. Ideas for this are addressed in the next tip.

# Tip #27

STORAGE > CURRENT > PENDING

There are many ways to create a home for pending papers, so I will share with you my personal system.

I've sorted my pending papers into plastic pockets by category (e.g. business, upcoming events, personal, receipts and coupons), and the plastic pockets reside in a magazine file by my desk. To see photos, product suggestions and other examples, go to https://www.the-organizing-boutique.com/organizing-paper-clutter.html.

# Tip #28

STORAGE > CURRENT

For current projects (business or personal alike), I suggest creating a file folder for each one and then storing them in a file sorter on your desk or in a desk file drawer. Either way, they are at your fingertips and you can access as well as file them away easily.

Personal projects could be anything that you're currently working on such as hobbies, crafts, putting together events, gift ideas for kids and so on. Business projects could be anything related to what you're currently working on during the day as well as job-hunting stuff and side gigs.

# <u>Tip #29</u>

STORAGE > CURRENT

For tax papers, keep 2 current folders:

- One for the current year so you can easily file related paper and access it at tax return time

- One for the information that is necessary every year like copies of a W-9 and a running list of documents you have to gather every year to do your tax returns

To see my list, go to https://www.the-organizing-boutique.com/organizing-your-taxes.html. Completed tax returns will be filed with the archival stuff and will be covered in the next section.

# Tip #30

STORAGE > CURRENT

I suggest using binders for storing paper that is helpful on the move.

For example, we have a binder for our dog. Inside are pockets for each category of paper (e.g. insurance, vet), and I can take it with me to the vet so that all of her records are handy.

This method would also be useful for children. Create a binder for each child, so that all important information is at your finger tips when you go to the doctor and so on.

More examples of papers helpful on the go could include documents related to moving homes, business papers that travel with you (e.g. to meetings, to clients, etc.), information related to pregnancy and medical records (if you frequent a doctor's office).

To check out my binder product suggestions (like the binder pockets I use), go to https://www.the-organizing-boutique.com/organizing-paperwork.html.

# Tip #31

STORAGE > CURRENT

Another type of paper that benefits from binder-organization is the kind that you tend to "flip through." This could include takeout menus, recipes, manuals and certain kinds of memorabilia.

I don't usually store memorabilia in binders (which will be addressed later), but I found that the binder solution was good for a few select things such as my husband's published writing. I put each piece he wrote and published in a sheet protector, and now it's a nice book we can flip through.

I made another memory binder like this for a client's son who plays an instrument. He performs with his school as well as locally, so I put each concert program in a sheet protector. Now he's got this wonderful book of his nicely

preserved memories that he can look
through.

# <u>Tip #32</u>

STORAGE > CURRENT

Other papers that fall into the current category should be filed in an accessible file drawer, cart or cabinet. This includes things like medical records, house-related projects, membership information, financial information, hobbies and car-related papers.

**The key here is to file according to what makes the most sense to you.** The question I always ask my clients in this situation is, "How will you think to find this later?"

For example, in my home we have a medical folder for each family member because we don't need more than that. Whereas one of my clients has several medical folders, one for each doctor she visits, one for her personal records and so on. That makes sense for her, because she's got a lot more going on

medically and therefore a lot more
relevant paper. Thus, do what makes
the most sense for your situation.

Start with a general folder for each
category, and then break it down as
necessary as the contents grow
assuming they all need to be kept.

For example:

- One medical folder for each
  family member
- One folder for house-related
  work (remember the title and
  other really important house
  documents will be in the
  archived files)
- One folder for memberships
  and then separate them each
  out when it becomes too full
- One folder for each financial
  account
- One folder for each car

If you are having trouble with this
and have a specific question, feel
free to send me an email

([Nealey@the-organizing-boutique.com](mailto:Nealey@the-organizing-boutique.com)).

# Tip #33

STORAGE > ARCHIVAL

Archival papers are not relevant now, but it is necessary to keep them for referencing later. This refers to things like taxes, legal papers, house documents and memorabilia.

# Tip #34

STORAGE > ARCHIVAL

Since they are archival, they don't need to be at your fingertips and can be filed out of the way. That said, you still need to be able to find and access them without any trouble. For example, this could be a filing cabinet in the basement rather than a bunch of unlabeled, stacked file boxes.

# <u>Tip #35</u>

STORAGE > ARCHIVAL >
MEMORABILIA

Memorabilia-related paper can be
filed in 3 ways:

- In binders (like we discussed
  earlier)
- In file folders
- In portfolios

A file folder holds all paper that is
8.5"x11" or smaller, and a portfolio
holds all of the bigger paper like child
artwork or large certificates. Start
with one of each for each family
member. If/when necessary, break
the file folders down into categories
and/or use more than one portfolio.

For example, your child could have
multiple memory files like one for
prized schoolwork, one for camp
memories, one for cherished cards
and letters and so on. You could
have multiple memory files like one

for things related to your childhood, your college years, your wedding, your children and so on.

Before you add a file or a portfolio however, sort through the memories that you kept to be sure that they are all worth keeping.

There's more about decluttering memorabilia in the next tip, but a quick example would be a child's artwork. At the end of the year, you may have mountains of paper with scribbles on them. Keep the ones that mean the most to you and let the others go to make room for the upcoming year.

To see portfolio suggestions and other memorabilia storage solutions, go to https://www.the-organizing-boutique.com/storage-for-kids.html.

# Tip #36

STORAGE > ARCHIVAL >
MEMORABILIA

One thing to note is that memories
can fade. At the time you are filing
something you may consider it to be
memorabilia, but when you come
back to it later you may not even
remember why you kept it.

Here are 2 suggestions in regards to
this.

First, when saving something like a
newspaper or magazine, be sure to
mark why it's important to you. If you
can't remember why you saved
something, then why store it?

Second, I know going through
memorabilia is probably one of the
last things on the organizing priority
list, but if the memories start to take
up too much space go through them.
You will find that with time, some
things you considered treasure are

now things you can let go.

This works especially well if you take a picture of it, so you essentially still have the memory but can let the physical paper go. (This also works for non-paper bulky memory items.)

# Tip #37

STORAGE > ARCHIVAL > TAXES

Completed tax returns and supporting documentation are also considered archival. The simplest method is to file each tax return with its related papers in a folder labeled by year. If your archival files are in a filing cabinet in the basement, then I would dedicate a drawer to tax stuff and file the most recent year in front.

# Tip #38

STORAGE > ARCHIVAL >
IMPORTANT DOCUMENTS

Another type of archival paper is
what I call the important document,
and it's something you keep forever.

This refers to legal papers,
passports, social security cards, birth
certificates, wills, powers of attorney,
debt information, estate stuff,
insurance documents, titles,
adoption information and so on.

These are the papers that you want
to keep in a fire-resistant box in case
something happens to your home AS
WELL AS back up digitally.

An easy way to keep these papers
organized in the fire-resistant box is
to sort them into binder pockets by
category. This way you can grab
them in a pinch, and they'll still be
organized.

For more details on what documents to store in a fire-resistant box, consult your attorney or accountant and/or check out this quick Google search (for "what papers to keep in a fire box) at https://www.google.com/search?q=what+papers+to+keep+in+a+fire+box&ie=utf-8&oe=utf-8.

# A Note From The Author

**To jump right in and bust through those paper piles, download the paper decluttering cheat sheet that supplements this book for free at https://www.the-organizing-boutique.com/paper-decluttering-cheat-sheet.html.**

Hey there! Did you enjoy this book? My hope is that you found it interesting, useful and motivating.

When I set out to write this book, my goal was to help people get through those paralyzing paper piles successfully by breaking down such an overwhelming project into doable, bite-sized tasks that can be immediately applied. Whether you got that out of reading this guide or you simply have one awesome takeaway, I'd love to hear about it.

I would kindly like to ask you to leave me an honest Amazon review. It can be short and sweet. Simply state one thought or feeling you took away after reading this book. Doing so not only spreads the word (which I immensely appreciate), but it also increases the possibility of helping someone else.

Thanks in advance and happy organizing!

# <u>Office</u>

(Because there's paper there too.)

# Tip #39

OFFICE

Everything we've talked about so far has referred to papers in the home, but all of the concepts apply to the office as well.

Action items may refer to tasks you need to get done for your boss, current papers may be your current work projects and archival papers may be completed projects that you want to refer to later.

Whatever your situation is, feel free to adapt the tips in this book to work for you.

# Tip #40

OFFICE

If you work from home like I do, then take the tips in this book and apply it to your work-related papers.

For example, I've got 2 file carts in my office for current papers – one is for personal and one is for business. My action items are sorted into pockets by category and stored by my desk in a magazine file, and I've got a pocket for business action items as well.

The key is to keep business paper filed separately from personal paper, so that you don't end up with huge piles of paper to sort that are a big mix of both.

# Tip #41

OFFICE

Speaking of office stuff let me take a quick minute to mention digital documents. Paper certainly isn't going anywhere at the moment, but we are living in a digital world (and I am a digital girl. I couldn't resist. LOL.).

What does your computer desktop look like?

Is it as cluttered as your physical desk?

Is it a sea of random documents that is overwhelming and confusing?

Can you find anything?

Just because it's digital doesn't mean it's not clutter, so it's important to organize your digital documents and also back them up. Here's a quick step-by-step of what to do along with my back up service recommendation at https://www.the-organizing-boutique.com/organizing-computer-files.html.

# Tip #42

OFFICE

Here's a quick word about scanning. Yes, scanning all of your paper would be a huge space saver. However, before you spend time researching options, spending the money on a scanner and thinking this will finally be the end of your paper piles, let me stop you. My intention isn't to burst your motivation bubble, but I do want steer you clear of a "fake" one.

I've witnessed it. The scanner is bought with the best of intentions and true excitement for the possibility of getting rid of so much paper clutter, but that's where it stops. Procrastination sets in (more on busting procrastination at https://www.the-organizing-boutique.com/ways-to-avoid-procrastination.html), because scanning in all of your paper is a MONSTER project. It's not unlike filing paper. Overwhelm takes

**76**

over, the scanning never happens
and the scanner just collects dust.

To avoid the waste of money, time
and hopefulness, my suggestion is to
start with a printer that has a
scanning feature. It's not high speed
but it will do the job good enough
until you know for sure if you are
what I would call "the scanning type."

The scanning types are the people
who actually use their high-speed
scanners almost daily. They have a
system down pat that includes
scanning papers in, a digital filing
system that ensures they know how
to name and find documents and a
discarding practice that means the
paper actually leaves their space.

If you discover that you are in fact
that type, then by all means,
purchase the nifty, high-speed
scanner. If not, utilize your 4-in-1
printer and your smart phone (e.g. I
use a scanning app called
GeniusScan) for the important stuff,

and put the tips in this book to good
use for the paper piles.

# A Note From The Author

**To jump right in and bust through those paper piles, download the paper decluttering cheat sheet that supplements this book for free at https://www.the-organizing-boutique.com/paper-decluttering-cheat-sheet.html.**

Hey there! Did you enjoy this book? My hope is that you found it interesting, useful and motivating.

When I set out to write this book, my goal was to help people get through those paralyzing paper piles successfully by breaking down such an overwhelming project into doable, bite-sized tasks that can be immediately applied. Whether you got that out of reading this guide or you simply have one awesome takeaway, I'd love to hear about it.

I would kindly like to ask you to leave me an honest Amazon review. It can be short and sweet. Simply state one thought or feeling you took away after reading this book. Doing so not only spreads the word (which I immensely appreciate), but it also increases the possibility of helping someone else.

Thanks in advance and happy organizing!

# MAINTENANCE

(Because this is the key to avoiding those mind-numbing, humungous decluttering sessions.)

# <u>Tip #43</u>

MAINTENANCE

Now that your paper has been through the initial round of decluttering and a storage system is in place, the last step is to do regular maintenance.

Maintenance is all about routines. It is IMPERATIVE to have systems in place to process incoming paper all the way through to its final destination. This is the ONLY way to keep your organization efforts up.

Otherwise, you're looking at going through another huge paper organizing project. The following tips give you some simple paper routines to implement.

# Tip #44

MAINTENANCE

This must be said, because the most organizational back sliding typically happens when it comes to maintenance. It's important to encourage yourself as much as possible.

The motivating question you can keep in mind is…a few minutes today or hours and hours later? This would be a good reminder to write on a post-it and stick in your line of sight at your desk along with one that says, "You got this."

# Tip #45

MAINTENANCE

Process paper (file or discard) as you go OR do it for an allotted period of time at the end of the day. It can be 5 minutes, or whatever time block makes sense for you, at the end of every day to maintain organization. This could mean clearing off your desk, the kitchen counter or whatever paper surfaced during the day that doesn't need to be out anymore.

# Tip #46

MAINTENANCE

The number one trick of the trade as far as maintenance is concerned is to deal with paper right away. This does not necessarily mean to do the action the paper requires right away, but rather to put the paper where it belongs immediately.

Typically, not knowing what to do with a piece of paper is what causes piles of clutter. However, if you follow the tips in this guide for giving each kind of paper a home as well as the maintenance routines, you'll know exactly where to put stuff and it won't take more than a minute.

And THAT, my friends, busts through procrastination faster than you can blink. (For the 10 common procrastination methods that keep us from getting organized and how to overcome them, go to https://www.the-organizing-boutique.com/

<u>ways-to-avoid-procrastination.html</u>).

# Tip #47

MAINTENANCE

One of the biggest sources of incoming paper is the mail, so it's critical to have a routine in place. This is mine. Feel free to use it or adapt it as necessary to fit your needs.

I get the mail out of the mailbox and sort through it immediately. As I go through it, I create piles of each category – recycle, shred, stuff I need to keep and my husband's mail. Then I put the recycling in our recycling bin, I shred the stuff with sensitive information on it (typically stuff like pre-approved credit card offers), I put my husband's mail in its proper home for him to go through and then I take care of the stuff I'm keeping.

The paper I keep either requires action or needs to be filed. If it needs to be filed, that happens right away.

If it requires action, I put it with my action papers. When we do get magazines or catalogs (it's rare but we occasionally get them), my husband's go in his mail pile and mine are put on the coffee table because I do most of my reading in the living room.

A few quick notes:

Notice how everything has a "home." My husband's mail, reading materials, action items, recycling, shredding, it all has a place where it belongs.

Also, right now, our household consists of just my husband and myself. Once we have kids, I will start employing something like a stacking letter tray so that each family member has an inbox for mail.

# Tip #48

MAINTENANCE

Another huge source of incoming paper is kid stuff like artwork, school papers and so on. It's important to have a routine for all kid paper work.

For artwork: Like mentioned in the storage section, let's say you have a file that holds art that is 8.5" x 11" pieces of paper and a portfolio for everything larger than that. At the end of the school year or when they are completely full (whichever comes first), go through them and keep only the best ones.

If you're hesitant about getting rid of any, take photos of the ones that aren't as good and then discard them. This way, you technically still have them without taking up any space.

Do the same thing for school papers like forms and completed work. Let's

say you have a bin or a file that you
gather school papers in throughout
the year. When it's full or the school
year is over (whichever comes first),
sort through it. Keep the best work,
the relevant forms and so on.

# Tip #49

MAINTENANCE

To stay organized at work, a paper routine is a must. Here are 3 samples of how a piece of paper can be processed.

First, the piece of paper comes in through the mail. It requires action, so you put it in the action tray on your desk and address it during the time block you allotted for doing action items. Once you complete the action, the piece of paper goes into the "upcoming" file until the event occurs. When it's the day of the event, you know just where to find that piece of paper.

Second, the piece of paper comes in through your email. You print it out and put it in the action tray until it gets done. Then it moves to one of the current project files and stays there until the project is complete. You decide it is something that needs to be referenced in the future, so it gets moved to the archives with completed project documents.

Third, a colleague gives a piece of paper to you. It requires action, so you put it in the action tray. Once you complete the action required, it moves to the "pending" file until others have done their part. When others complete their action, you decide to recycle the piece of paper since it is done and does not need to be referenced later.

# Tip #50

MAINTENANCE

It's time to celebrate (and not just because you've almost finished this book)!

Rewarding yourself after accomplishing goals like decluttering your paper is an important part of the process. It keeps you motivated, and getting short-term rewards is exactly what the procrastination monster yearns for.

Why not use it to our advantage in a way in which the procrastination doesn't win?

Set small and/or large milestones throughout your project, decide on an appropriate reward for each one and don't forget to schedule these celebrations so that they actually occur.

For example, you could set a small

milestone of sticking with the decluttering part for 2 weeks and then gift yourself a bottle of wine or a nice dinner at your favorite restaurant. You could also decide to set a large milestone of having no piles on any surfaces anywhere and gift yourself a massage or a spa day.

No matter what you decide, just make sure that celebrations and rewards of some kind are built in to your process. Besides, you deserve it and it makes this whole thing a lot more fun.

# **<u>Conclusion</u>**

(So…how are you feeling after
reading all the tips in this book?)

Motivated? I hope you are at least a
little bit determined. The tips in this
book are meant to be so simple that
you feel like you could take action
this very moment. **The key is to
take that action one micro step at
a time on a consistent basis**. Read
that last sentence again for good
measure; it's really, really important.

Overwhelmed? That's natural. There
is a lot of information in this book, so
take some time to digest it. Then
figure out where you want to start,
put on your motivational music
(Boom boom bah! Boom boom bah!
We will, we will, rock you!) and jump
in like the rock star I know you are.

Anxious to get started because you
simply cannot look at those paper
piles one second longer?! Alright!
Let's do this.

The first thing you can do is download this free one-page cheat sheet to keep on hand as you declutter your paper piles rather than having to flip through all the pages in this book (http://www.the-organizing-boutique.com/paper-decluttering-cheat-sheet.html). Also, there's a resource page at the end with all the links that were mentioned throughout the book, so be sure to check that out.

Then, you pick up a piece of paper...but the cycle won't stop there anymore.

Hooray! You pick up that piece of paper with determination, confidence and the conviction to follow this thing through using this guide and the cheat sheet to make a decision about its fate. You're in charge; you have the power. Rock star, superhero, whatever awesomeness you see yourself as, wield the ability like you own this piece of paper (because, in fact, you do).

I'm not physically there with you, so how this ends is entirely up to you. Although after reading this book, I'm hoping that my words will stay with you as you get organized.

The important thing to remember is that the ONLY way this is going to happen is if you take action regularly, and keep the procrastination monster disarmed and disinterested. Thus, I'll let you finish this sentence, hopefully with a different ending than the story you were telling before you read this book.

You pick up a piece of paper…

P.S. I can't help myself. Here are some awesome endings to choose from or to draw inspiration from. Feel free to print these out and put them up in a visual place.

You pick up a piece of paper, and make a decision faster than a superhero with super speed saving the day.

You pick up a piece of paper, and fire
that thing like a boss.

You pick up a piece of paper and
shred it like a rock star does on a
guitar, and the crowd goes wild.

You pick up a piece of paper, and
rule that thing like a king or queen.
Either way, you wear the crown.

# A Note From The Author

****To jump right in and bust through those paper piles, <u>download the paper decluttering cheat sheet that supplements this book for free at https://www.the-organizing-boutique.com/paper-decluttering-cheat-sheet.html</u>.****

Hey there! Did you enjoy this book? My hope is that you found it interesting, useful and motivating.

When I set out to write this book, my goal was to help people get through those paralyzing paper piles successfully by breaking down such an overwhelming project into doable, bite-sized tasks that can be immediately applied. Whether you got that out of reading this guide or you simply have one awesome takeaway, I'd love to hear about it.

I would kindly like to ask you to leave me an honest Amazon review. It can be short and sweet. Simply state one thought or feeling you took away after reading this book. Doing so not only spreads the word (which I immensely appreciate), but it also increases the possibility of helping someone else.

Thanks in advance and happy organizing!

# Resources

The Paper Decluttering Cheat Sheet
(Free Supplement To This Book)
https://www.the-organizing-
boutique.com/paper-decluttering-cheat-
sheet.html


The Procrastinator's Guide To Getting
Organized
https://www.the-organizing-
boutique.com/ways-to-avoid-
procrastination.html


List Of Papers To Shred
https://www.the-organizing-
boutique.com/shredding-paper.html


How To Organize Bills & Action Items
https://www.the-organizing-
boutique.com/monthly-bill-organizer.html


Organizing Paperwork That's Pending
https://www.the-organizing-
boutique.com/organizing-paper-
clutter.html

# About Nealey Stapleton

Nealey Stapleton is a professional organizer, an author, a small business owner, a DIY blogger, an adoring wife, a Pug lover, a hula hooping guru, a cheese addict and a happy napper.

Do you want to hang out with Nealey? Join her community online via The-Organizing-Boutique.com.